$\frac{1.00}{5}$

# EXPLORE MICHIGAN

## DETROIT

George Cantor has been a journalist in the Detroit area for more than 40 years. He worked for the *Detroit Free Press* and the *Detroit News* as a baseball writer, travel writer, reporter and columnist.

His proudest achievements were covering the 1968 Detroit Tigers in their championship season, raising two beautiful daughters and seeing columns he had written years ago still hanging on refrigerator doors around the state.

He also has written 15 books on sports, travel and history.

George and his wife Sherry are residents of West Bloomfield, along with their irascible west highland terrier, Charlie.

# EXPLORE MICHIGAN

## DETROIT

An Insider's Guide to Michigan

George Cantor

The University of Michigan Press
Ann Arbor
&
Petoskey Publishing Company
Traverse City

2008   2007   2006   2005   4   3   2   1

9397    ISBN 0-472-03092-2

Library of Congress Cataloging-in-publication Data on File

Explore Michigan: Detroit
Reviewed by Stacey Duford and
Charles Ferguson Barker

Cover photograph provided by
Marge Beaver, Photography Plus
www.photography-plus.com

Inside photography courtesy of
Detroit Chamber of Commerce

# CONTENTS

| | |
|---|---|
| Don't Miss List | 7 |
| The Turf | 9 |
| The Towns | 12 |
| Local Color | 13 |
| Where to Stay | 20 |
| Eating Out | 24 |
| City Walks | 29 |
| A City Drive | 38 |
| Along the River to Lake St. Clair | 41 |
| Shopping | 45 |
| Museums | 50 |
| Country Walks | 59 |
| Golf | 61 |
| After Dark | 64 |
| Casinos | 69 |
| Best with Kids | 72 |
| Annual Events | 73 |

*Explore Michigan: An Insider's Guide to Michigan* is not meant to be a complete listing of every restaurant or every shop; it is truly meant to be an "insider's" guide. It recommends the places that the locals, and in the case of the tourist areas, long-time summer residents, know about, frequent and recommend to their family and friends.

For example, in Traverse City, the parking meters have a button that you can hit for thirty free minutes. In Leelanau County, the National Park Service conducts winter snowshoe tours of the park. In Detroit, there are cozy restaurants that out-of-towners rarely find. And if you want a more affordable, and quiet weekend at the Grand Hotel on Mackinac Island, it is now open in early spring.

Author George Cantor has been writing travel books for over twenty years. A life-long Michigander, he has traveled and explored Michigan with the gusto it takes to make these books special. Though they are guidebooks, they make for a good read before, during and after you plan to visit. George also wanted to make sure that he really had the local flare for each book in this series, so he agreed to have locals review each book and give their comments to him.

The result is *Explore Michigan: An Insider's Guide to Michigan*, where the aerial photographs on the covers by exceptionally talented Marge Beaver invite you in. Once you start reading, you are on your way to invaluable information that puts you on the inside of what our great state has to offer.

--the publishers

# DETROIT AND WAYNE COUNTY

## *The Top Ten Don't Miss List*

1. Stroll into the past at the Henry Ford Museum and Greenfield Village, Dearborn.
2. See where the sound of the 60s was born at the Motown Museum.
3. Watch the traffic on the country's busiest inland waterway, the Detroit River, from Hart Plaza or Belle Isle.
4. See how they build a car on Ford's Rouge Plant tour, Dearborn.
5. Take in a live performance at one of Detroit's many theaters.
6. Go across the river to Windsor for the view from Canada.
7. Capture a piece of Poland on a walk along Joseph Campau Street, Hamtramck.
8. Spend an hour or two among the great Italian Renaissance and American collections at the Detroit Institute of Arts.
9. Drive out Lake Shore through the Grosse Pointes to the Edsel and Eleanor Ford House.
10. Sample a bit of the Middle East on W. Warren Avenue, Dearborn.

# THE TURF

People who are not comfortable with big cities approach them with caution. All big cities have good places and bad, and Detroit has had its share of bad headlines, but don't let that stop you from exploring this city. Detroit has much to offer.

Visitors are usually surprised, and even charmed, by the city. Its wealth of cultural attractions. Its scenic riverside setting. The genuine friendliness of its people. The nearness of Canada, just across the river. The graciousness of its historic neighborhoods and suburbs. It is also a sports-besotted place, with the Tigers at Comerica Park, the Lions at Ford Field and the Red Wings at Joe Louis Arena, all located downtown. (Basketball's Pistons play in the Palace of Auburn Hills,
in Oakland County.)

There is no getting around the fact that in some places Detroit resembles a wasteland where the wheels came off Western civilization. In the places where tourists are likely to go, however, it is as safe as any large American city and incomparably better than it was a decade ago.

Because of its standing as an industrial behemoth, Detroit is perceived as a product of the automotive age. It is actually much older, one of the first outposts established by the French on the Great Lakes.

The city traces its roots back to 1701, when Antoine de la Mothe Cadillac and a small party of settlers arrived from Quebec to establish a fort. It was meant to guard one of the essential water passages of the fur trade. Detroit, in fact, means "The Strait," and its location was the nexus between the Upper and Lower Great Lakes.

For almost 200 years it existed as a place of middling importance. England replaced France as its overlord, and then the Americans arrived. The fur trade waned, replaced by lumbering as the major economic force. Michigan was carved out of the Northwest Territory to form a state.

By the end of the 19th Century, Detroit was a gracious

community with tree-lined streets and a few small, prosperous industries; carriages and stoves. The chamber of commerce boasted it was a place "where life is worth living."

Then Henry Ford drove his little car through the downtown streets and everything changed. For the first two decades of the new century, this was America's ultimate boomtown. Its population doubled and then doubled again, so that by 1920 it numbered at around one million.

There seemed to be no end to the well-paying jobs here and men came from around the world to claim them. When Ford announced his revolutionary "Five-dollar day" in 1914, they flocked to his plant in Highland Park. They came from the played out lumber camps in the north woods, from the Southern highlands, from Poland and Italy and Hungary and Russia. By 1920, Detroit had the highest percentage of foreign born residents of any city in the country. And still they came.

Entire neighborhoods were built almost overnight, only to be replaced by almost identical ones a little farther out. The city is flat as a board, with no geographic impediments to its expansion. There was no time for planning, no room for orderly growth. It was a wild rush to put up enough housing to hold the new arrivals.

The Depression slowed the pace. With its economic dependence on a manufacturing base, Detroit was savaged by the downturn worse than most cities. But in the 40s, it roared back to life as the Arsenal of Democracy, its auto plants converted to wartime industry. The influx of job seekers resumed, many of them African-Americans, and by 1950 the city had close to two million residents.

Its suburbs shared in the growth. Dearborn was the home of the Ford Motor Co. and its massive Rouge plant was the largest industrial complex in the world. Steel and glass came in at one end and were driven away at the other as an automobile.

Chrysler was based in Highland Park and its Dodge plant dominated the community of Hamtramck. Massive Chevrolet and Cadillac factories were in the city itself, as were Packard and Nash and DeSoto.

Then it started to turn around. As prosperity grew, the second generation of auto workers began looking to the suburbs of Oakland and Macomb counties for newer homes with bigger backyards, and a garage in which to park the machines they had made. The industry itself began to decentralize. Freeway construction uprooted settled neighborhoods, especially black ones, and changed the racial texture of the city.

By the 1960s, Detroit was perceived as a city in decline, and the riots of 1967 sealed the deal. A slow middle class exodus turned into a headlong rush for the exits. The homicide rate reached levels not seen since the 1920s, when gangs battled over the liquor trade from Canada. Most of

*Stadiums, skyline and a reborn downtown*

the new death toll was drug related and not random. But that was small consolation and did little to stop the outmigration.

Detroit has lost more than one million people since its population peaked, and it shows. In recent years, however, there has been a substantial revitalization of its downtown. Casinos, stadiums, restored theaters, new corporate headquarters, a renewed appreciation of its historic buildings.

The city isn't what it once was. But the city that now is taking shape is worth seeing.

# THE TOWNS

**Detroit.** The tenth largest city in America, and the only one ever to exceed one million in population and then fall below that figure again. It also has the largest percentage of African-American residents of any big city.

The place radiates outward from the Detroit River in a roughly fan-shaped street arrangement with a grid superimposed over it. Sure, it's confusing, and to make matters worse public transportation ranges from poor to nonexistent. But almost everyone takes the freeways to get where they're going.

Woodward Avenue is the main street. It divides the city's East and West sides and connects downtown with the other signature districts in the city's core: The Medical Center and Cultural Center, with its museums, and Wayne State University campus. The New Center, the former home base of General Motors, was planned by the company as the first business district in the country to stand apart from a traditional downtown. Ironically, GM has relocated its headquarters back to downtown.

**Dearborn.** The location of the world-class facilities of the Henry Ford Museum-Greenfield Village complex. Ford was born on a farm in this community, built his estate here and opened the Rouge plant here, too. It is still the headquarters of the corporation he founded.

Dearborn is also home to one of the largest Arab-American communities in America.

**Grosse Pointe.** This is where much of the automotive wealth found its home. There are actually five communities that share the name---the Park, the Farms, the Shores, the Woods and Grosse Pointe itself. They line up along Lake St. Clair in regal splendor, the symbol of making it big in the Motor City.

**Hamtramck.** It is no longer the cozy Polish enclave it used to be. But this little community, entirely surrounded by Detroit, retains a strong ethnic sense in its shops, tidy houses, churches and eating places.

**Plymouth.** A slice of small town America preserved at the edge of the city, in the midst of the area's most rapid growth. A town square, old homes, little shops. It's as if it all just emerged from a 1950s cocoon, which makes it a wonderful place for an aimless stroll.

**Windsor.** The tranquil Canadian city across the river. It is also an auto town, but has managed to keep its downtown vibrant and its riverside lined with gracious parks. It is a distinct change of pace from the sprawling American city, although it does have a wild side with its notorious strip clubs.

**Wyandotte.** Downriver is the name given to the suburbs, many of them heavily industrial, south of the city. Wyandotte
is the center of this area. It features a pleasant, compact downtown and some nice parks along the water. It is also a point of departure for a driving trip around Grosse Ile, an upscale island suburb with some magnificent and historic homes on the water.

# LOCAL COLOR

### *Henry Ford*

Ford was a cantankerous, bigoted genius. A visionary who never really outgrew his farmhouse roots.

He, Ford, revolutionized the manufacturing concepts of the entire world, and in return the world made him one of its wealthiest men. Foreign statesmen undertook pilgrimages to his Highland Park factory to observe first-hand the miracle he had wrought. He did not invent the assembly line or the automobile. But he was the first to understand how the one could be applied to the other.

Ford campaigned for peace in the midst of World War I, and at one time was considered a serious presidential possibility. Yet he also financed a scurrilous anti-Semitic newspaper that was eagerly read by the likes of the young Adolf Hitler.

Ford probably did more than any other individual to erase the rural, isolated world of mid-19th Century America. Then he did all he could to try and recreate that world in idealized form in a museum setting just a few miles from his birthplace. Even in 2004, more than a century after his company was founded, a poll of corporate leaders by *Business Week* magazine named Ford the most innovative businessman in American history.

A man of strong ideas and puzzling contradictions, he also did more to shape modern Detroit than any other individual. The family name is on highways, hospitals, colleges, office buildings, stadiums.

Ford was a night shift engineer at the Detroit Edison Company in 1896. He was 33 years old, an inveterate tinkerer and dreamer, working in his every spare moment on something he called a quadricycle in the shed of his Detroit home. Then he rolled it onto Bagley Street one June night and, as he reported to his wife, Clara, "the darned thing ran."

It was not until 1903 that Ford was able to start up his first production plant. By that time Ransom Olds already had been turning out his cars in Detroit for four years. But Ford had bigger ideas.

He hired bicycle racer Barney Oldfield to drive his car in highly publicized speed events. Those record-breaking victories made Ford a household name. Oldfield was clocked at a mile a minute, an almost unbelievable speed for a motor vehicle at that time.

Then Ford began studying the assembly line techniques used in food processing plants. His first factories were unsuited to such a set-up and he asked architect Albert

Kahn to design a well-illuminated plant with vast amounts of interior space, so that the work could be brought to the workers.

The landmark Highland Park plant opened in 1910 and within three years it was turning out 250,000 cars a year at a production cost the industry had regarded as unattainable. The company's annual profits were $25 million.

Then Ford dropped the biggest bombshell of all---the $5 day for eight hours of work. That was twice the national standard for factory work. But Ford understood that he could expand his market exponentially by lifting the pay of his employees to the level of being able to afford the cars they made.

But that still wasn't enough. Ford envisioned a totally integrated complex, with all assembly components located on one level and on-site control of all material used in the manufacturing process. Again he turned to Kahn for the answer. The result was the Rouge Plant, a 1,100-acre industrial marvel that was the wonder of its times. And still is.

At his death in 1947, Ford had transformed industry, his hometown and the world. He passed away in his Dearborn estate, Fairlane, on the banks of the Rouge River. The river had flooded in heavy spring rains, cutting off electrical power to the house. In a candle-lit, wood-heated room, he passed away in a setting very much like the one in which he had entered the world he changed forever.

### *Joe Louis*

When he entered the ring at Yankee Stadium in June, 1938, Joe Louis was not an especially popular heavyweight champ.

In the nation's black communities he had been elevated to heroic status. On the nights of his fights one could walk the streets of Paradise Valley, Detroit's black neighborhood, and hear the radio broadcast of every punch coming from every open window.

He was a hometown idol, raised on the streets of this city.

Joe Louis Barrow was one of the guys and his triumphs were everyone's victories over poverty and the indignities of racism.

But the country at large was slow to warm to the second black man to hold the heavyweight title. When he fought Max Schmeling, the only boxer ever to defeat him until he came out of retirement, on this early summer night, however, he seemed to fight for America. Schmeling, whether fairly or not, had been promoted as Hitler's favorite, an example of what superior Aryan athletes could accomplish.

Louis' destruction of him in one round gave millions of Americans, frightened by what the Nazis were doing in Europe, new courage and hope. It was one of the symbolic sporting events in the nation's history and instantly transformed Louis into the greatest African-American hero of his era.

His uncomplaining service in World War II and appearances on behalf of the war effort confirmed his place in the hearts of his countrymen.

He still occupies that place in Detroit. The city's downtown athletic arena, home of hockey's Red Wings, bears his name. A statue of him in fighting pose is displayed in Cobo Hall, the main convention center.

More controversial is the Big Fist, mounted at the foot of the city's main street, Woodward Avenue. The 24-foot long sculpture, unveiled in 1986, was intended to symbolize the strength behind Louis' accomplishments. Many interpreted it, however, as an expression of black power in a racially divided city and wanted it taken down.

Time has not entirely taken the edge from that dispute. But the shining memory of Joe Louis is undimmed in his hometown.

## Albert Kahn

He was the architect of Detroit's greatest years; the man who designed its factories, its skyscrapers, many of its homes and public buildings.

"No other architectural firm had a greater influence on the development of industrial architecture than Albert Kahn's," wrote *Architectural Record* magazine. "But there is evidence that the architect's work had a wider influence, too, affecting the development of Modernism itself."

Kahn shrugged off such accolades. "I got all the breaks," he once said. "Nine-tenths of my success has come because I listened to what people said they wanted and gave it to them."

He is best known for listening to Henry Ford and giving him the landmark auto plants in Highland Park and the Rouge. These were vast, functional buildings. But he was also capable of designing the city's most graceful and ornate office tower, the Fisher Building, as well as the magnificent lakeside estate of Edsel and Eleanor Ford.

Kahn was born in Germany and arrived in Detroit in 1880 as an 11-year-old. His family was poor, and when he showed some talent as an artist he took the only available position---an unpaid apprenticeship at a top local architectural firm. He learned the basics, won scholarships to study abroad and by 1895 he was able to open his own office.

The commission that changed his life came nine years later. He was hired to build the main assembly plant for Packard Motors. He used reinforced concrete, a material that was coming into use in Europe but was still little known in America. The success of that factory, so much more open and cleaner than the usual industrial plant, made a deep impression on Ford. He hired Kahn immediately.

By his firm's count, Kahn worked on more than 1,000 commissions for Ford until Kahn's death in 1942. His last major job was the Willow Run bomber plant, part of the muscle of the Arsenal of Democracy that helped turn the tide of World War II.

But Kahn also left an indelible mark on the city itself.

The original General Motors headquarters, the Detroit Athletic Club, the *Detroit News* offices, Detroit Police Headquarters, dozens of others. All of them are still standing, part of a remarkable visual testament to his genius.

## Berry Gordy

*Where the Motown sound was born*

When he opened his recording studio in 1959, in an old house on the city's fading West Grand Boulevard, Berry Gordy immediately put up a sign over the front door. "Hitsville, USA" it said.

The neighbors guffawed, and for good reason. For a young black man, with no particular expertise in the music business and a distinct shortage of working capital, to think he could break into the record industry seemed ludicrous.

Black musical artists were well established by this time. Money and control, however, was all white. But Gordy had a secret sauce, a sound. A fresh, urban beat that pounded away like the rhythm he had heard in the auto factories of his hometown.

Within a few years, the Motown Sound would sweep across America and Europe and change popular music forever.

Gordy had started up his new Tamla label at a propitious

time. The payola scandals--disc jockeys taking bribes to play certain records--had just rocked the recording industry. With threats of legal action in the air, radio stations suddenly were more receptive to listening to unknown artists on lesser labels.

Gordy was able to give them music worth listening to. Within two years, he had his first national hit. An old friend, Smokey Robinson, recorded one of his own compositions, "Shop Around," and it rose to number two on the charts. A few months later, the Marvelettes went all the way to the top with "Please, Mr. Postman."

It was another girl group, the Supremes, who really put the Gordy enterprise over the top. Glamorous, chic and talented, the three singers became the top act in the country by the mid 60s.

Then the hits and the groups just kept on coming; the wealth of talent that Gordy always knew lay in urban black neighborhoods. The Temptations. The Four Tops. Martha and the Vandellas. Marvin Gaye, from Washington, D.C. Stevie Wonder, from Flint. The Jackson 5, from Gary, Indiana. It turned out that "Hitsville" was too modest a description of what had been achieved in the house on West Grand Boulevard.

Gordy decided that he had accomplished all he could in Detroit and moved his company to Los Angeles in 1971. Many of the artists remain in the area, however. And the sound they created still lingers in the streets and in the hearts of this city.

### *"Mad" Anthony Wayne*

The man who gave his name to Michigan's most populous county barely set foot in the area. His military genius, however, finally drove the British out of Detroit in 1796, a matter of 13 years after they had promised to leave in the treaty that ended the Revolutionary War.

Wayne had won his nickname for his audacity as a general in that conflict. He was given the responsibility for taking well-defended British fortifications at Stony Point in

1779 on a critical stretch of the Hudson River. George Washington asked him if it could be taken by a surprise attack at night. "General," Wayne responded, "I'll storm Hell if you only plan it." Wayne carried off the seemingly impossible task and from then on he was Mad Anthony.

Fifteen years later, Washington turned to him again. An American army sent up from Cincinnati to capture Detroit in 1791 had been wiped out by an Indian force, one of the worst defeats by percentage of casualties in U.S. military history. Wayne was sent to Ohio to repair the damage, and after three years of preparation he began his offensive. He deflected every assault on his force, and in the summer of 1794, at Fallen Timbers, outside present-day Toledo, won a decisive victory.
His army entered Detroit less than two years later, and Michigan and western Ohio had been secured for American settlers.

On his way back to his home in Philadelphia for a hero's welcome, he took sick and died in Erie, Pa. Wayne County, organized to include virtually all of the Lower Peninsula of the future state of Michigan and much of northern Ohio, was named for him that same year.

# WHERE TO STAY

## *Top of the Line*

**Ritz-Carlton.** Dearborn. M-39 (Southfield Freeway Service Drive) between Ford Road and Michigan Avenue. (313) 441-2000. (888) 709-8081.

The local outpost of the luxury hotel brand. Convenient to Ford World Headquarters, just across the freeway, as well as Fairlane Town Center and the Henry Ford Museum complex.

Some complain the chain is getting a little stodgy, with its haute British tone and hunting scenes on the walls in the lobby and restaurants. Still, the accommodations and service are excellent and this continues to be the approved address for those with business in Dearborn. Downtown Detroit is just 15 minutes away and some visitors with business there prefer the more convenient shopping opportunities in this area.

There are 308 rooms and a heated indoor pool.

**Hyatt-Regency.** Dearborn. Southfield Freeway at Michigan Avenue. (313) 593-1234. (800) 233-1234.

A visually striking building, with its 13-story curved glass front, this is also a top choice for those doing business with Ford or touring the nearby museums. A bit less formal than the Ritz and somewhat less expensive, too. It is more than twice as large, however, with 772 rooms. It also has an indoor heated pool.

**Detroit Marriott Renaissance Center.** W. Jefferson Avenue in the RenCen. (313) 568-8000. (800) 352-0831.

This 73-story cylindrical tower is the tallest building in Detroit, with spectacular views over the city, the river and into Canada. The rooms are wedge-shaped and not overly large, and the complex itself is a bit confusing to navigate.

Still, this is the epicenter of the city and the headquarters for General Motors. While the RenCen has never quite lived up to the city-saving hype that accompanied its opening in the late 1970s, it is also the visual signature of Detroit. There are 1,298 rooms.

**The Atheneum.** Detroit. Brush at E. Lafayette Street. (313) 962-2323. (800) 772-2323.

A boutique hotel, with just 174 units, most of them one-bedroom suites. It is linked by internal passageway with the Greektown entertainment district and is just a short walk from the new stadiums of the Detroit Tigers and Lions and the Harmonie Park theater and restaurant area. This is a striking 10-story building with a theme reminiscent of classical Greece.

*Sleeping with History*

**The Inn on Ferry Street.** Detroit. Ferry, just east of Woodward in the Cultural Center area. (313) 871-6000. This was the city's most fashionable address in the 1880s and 1890s and several of its wealthiest citizens built their homes here. It later become the preferred neighborhood of Jewish and then black professionals.

By the 1970s, however, ownership had passed to Wayne State University which planned to tear the houses down for new classrooms. A group called Preservation Wayne managed to fend off that destruction, and several of the historic houses are now linked to make this unique city property.

There are 42 rooms in four different 19th Century homes, each of them distinct in architectural style. A good location for those visiting the university, the museums of the Cultural Center or the Medical Center.

**Dearborn Inn.** 20301 Oakwood Blvd., north from the Oakwood exit of M-39 (Southfield Freeway). (313) 271-2700. (800)352-0831.

Built by Henry Ford in 1931 for the convenience of visitors to his auto empire and museums, the inn is modeled on the colonial style he favored. A few detached cottages are furnished as tributes to famous Americans.

Marriott has taken over management of the 222-room hotel and introduced several upgrades in the rooms, restaurants and public areas. But it is meant to reflect the style of an earlier era and those preferring a more modern setting, may be uncomfortable here.

The inn's Ten Eyck's Tavern, incidentally, is a tribute to one of the state's earliest restaurants, a coaching stop on the old Chicago Road. According to legend, the proprietor used to joke that the steaks he served came from wolves. When one young lady heard that, she responded, "That must make me a wolverine." The story circulated so widely that the entire state soon became known by that nickname, including the University of Michigan athletic teams.

**Omni Detroit Riverplace.** South of E. Jefferson Avenue by way of McDougall. (313) 259-9500. (800) 843-6664.

A small hotel, east of downtown, in the midst of the restored Parke-Davis complex on the Detroit River. Most of the buildings here were put up between 1890 and 1920 when Parke-Davis was among the largest pharmaceutical firms in America. It was the first to devise a method for standardizing doses and came up with treatments for diphtheria and epilepsy.

After the company went out of business it was sold to a developer in 1982 and the buildings converted to offices, restaurants and residences.

Parke-Davis chose this site for ease in shipping and the 108-room hotel puts you as close to the water as you can get in the city. It is new construction which successfully matches the style of the surrounding historic structures.

### *Staying with Kids*

**Hampton Inn Dearborn.** 20061 Michigan Avenue. (313) 436-9600. Just west of the Southfield Freeway. (800) 426-7866.

Close to the Henry Ford Museum, shopping and movies at Fairlane Center, and lots of restaurants in downtown Dearborn. Heated indoor pool.

### *At Metro Airport*

**Westin Hotel.** In the McNamara Terminal Building. (734) 942-6500. (800) 228-3000.

It couldn't be a more convenient location, and this hotel is a fine complement to the airport's new terminal, which opened in 2002. Direct passage to the ticket counters, indoor pool, and nice luxury touches all around.

*In Livonia*

**Livonia Marriott.** 17100 Laurel Park Drive.
(734) 462-3100. (800) 352-0831. Off I-275 at Six Mile Road.
Part of the Laurel Park office and shopping complex
and a convenient address for those visiting the western
Wayne County suburbs.

# EATING OUT

### *Seven Dinners in Detroit*

**Rattlesnake Club.** In the River Place complex, east of
downtown. South of E. Jefferson, to the end of Joseph
Campau. (313) 567-4400. Nice river views and an inventive
menu created by Chef Jimmy Schmidt. The style is
"Contemporary American," the surroundings are understa-
ted elegance and the experience is always satisfying. Many
of the customers consider themselves aggressively hip, but
they can be safely ignored.

**The Whitney.** 4421 Woodward Avenue north of
downtown. (313) 832-5700. In a stately, splendidly restored
1894 mansion built with big lumber money, dinner is a production here. Try the duck or the lamb chops. Then retire to
one of the smaller, allegedly haunted rooms upstairs for
dessert and entertainment.

**Sweet Georgia Brown.** 1045 Brush at Monroe, in the
Greektown area of downtown. (313) 965-1245. The top
spot for people-watching in the city, where local professionals go for a swell night out and classic southern cuisine. The
fried lobster is masterful, and all the seafood dishes hit the
mark. And then there's sweet potato pie, double chocolate
cake and a raft of other desserts that will send your carbs
meter berserk.

**Cuisine.** 670 Lothrop, across from the Fisher Theatre, in the New Center. (313) 872-5110. A favorite with theater-goers, this is a restaurant that can stand on its own merits. Set in an early 20th Century house, the menu takes some of the French standards and dresses them up with unexpected pairings---such as beef with seared foie gras. A place to experiment with your palate.

**La Dolce Vita.** 17546 Woodward, in the Palmer Park area, six miles north of downtown. (313) 865-0331. A little out of the way, this is a little jewel box, with new perspectives on the basic Italian cookbook. Knockout gnocchi, and you can't go wrong with either the veal or chicken piccata. A friendly, cosmopolitan staff makes the experience fun, too.

**Atlas Global Bistro.** 3111 Woodward, north of downtown. (313) 831-2241. Not in the most attractive of urban neighborhoods, this place chooses the whole world as its dining neighborhood. The menu may feature dishes from Spain or India or Thailand—depending upon the season and the mood. It's in an old storefront, with big glass windows looking out onto Woodward. But the big attraction looks towards the inner person.

**Roma Café.** 3401 Riopelle, in the Eastern Market. (It is hard to find if you don't know the territory. Best advice is to cab it.) (313) 831-5940. Detroiters love it for sentimental reasons. It's the oldest restaurant in the city, going strong for over a century at the edge of the former Italian neighborhood. Sure, it's old fashioned and if you hit it at the wrong time you may get the feeling that they're throwing the food at you. But they know their way around the sauces here and, hey, it's a piece of history.

## Seven Dinners in Suburban Wayne County

**Mackinnon's.** 126 E. Main, Northville. (248) 348-1991. Fine dining in an old fashioned downtown, in the northwestern corner of Wayne County. Excellent steaks and an everchanging assortment of imaginatively prepared game dishes, including blown-up duck. Don't ask, just try it.

**La Bistecca.** 39405 Plymouth Road, Plymouth. (734) 254-0400. Lean, Piedmontese beef is the specialty in this Italian steak house. The menu ranges far beyond the basics, with a nicely conceived assortment of appetizers. But that 20-ounce porterhouse is hard to resist, if your tummy is empty and your wallet is full.

**Emily's.** 505 N. Center, Northville. (248) 349-0505. This old house is short of glitter, but some would argue the food is the best in the area. Chef Rick Halberg presents a changing selection of country French dishes, mostly drawn from Provence and Perigord. The pace is leisurely, the results often spectacular from its limited menu.

**Moro's.** 6535 Allen Road. Allen Park. (313) 382-7152. The Italian fundamentals are here, with just a hint of Hungarian and Macedonian overtones. For example, along with the veal marsala you can also get a paprikas. Its flaming desserts are worth waiting for and were featured on the Food Network.

**Fonte d'Amore.** 32020 Plymouth Road, Livonia. (734) 422-0770. Good, straightforwarding, reasonably priced Italian cooking in a nice, straightforwarding suburban neighborhood. The Del Signore family named the place after their hometown. It means Fountain of Love and the setting may get a wee bit kitschy. Kudos for the way the basics are done.

**Da Edoardo.** 19767 Mack, Grosse Pointe Woods. (313) 881-8540. A dependable, time-tested place in an area noted more for stay-at-home or at-the-club dining. A whiff of 60s glamour is still apparent in the banquettes and soft lights. But the saltimbocca and gnocchi are right on time. A branch of this family-run operation is located in the Fox Theatre building in downtown Detroit, right across the street from Comerica Park. It, too, is worth a visit.

**Café Bon Homme.** 844 Penniman, Plymouth. (734) 453-6260. Tucked away in a downtown corner of a picturesque community, this is a high end bistro with some Asian and contemporary American touches. Intimate, with several artsy touches, and a seafood bisque over which the local food critics wear out their adjectives.

### *Informal Places*

**Lafayette Coney Island.** (313) 964-8198. It's a Detroit original, on the corner of West Lafayette and Michigan Avenue, in the heart of downtown. Chili slathered over a hot dog is the big attraction and everyone in the city has probably wandered through its doors at one time or another. Why Coney Island in the heart of Michigan? Who cares. Just dig in.

**Sindbads.** 100 St. Clair Street, on the Detroit River. (313) 822-8000. A perennial boaters' favorite, located on a marina with views of the water from its upstairs deck. Featuring the all-time Great Lakes favorite, perch, along with terrific burgers and a formidable steak sandwich. Summertime lines go out the door on weekends.

**Polish Village.** 2990 Yemans, Hamtramck. (313) 874-5726. Food like your grandma used to make. City chicken (rolled pork on a stick), kielbasa, pierogi and all that artery-clogging good stuff. In the heart of an old Polish neighborhood, in a hearty, friendly, noisy room.

**La Shish.** 12198 N. Michigan, Dearborn.
(313) 584-4477. Middle-Eastern delights so good it started a
chain throughout the area. But this is the original, and if you've
never tried lamb shwarma with hummous, hurry on down and
try it here. Incredible fruit juice concoctions, too.

**Xochimilco.** Bagley at 23rd Street. West of downtown.
(313) 843-0179. Everyone has their own favorite in Detroit's
expanding Mexican neighborhood. But this is the consensus
choice, a warren of little rooms serving Tex-Mex cuisine and a
few authentic dishes from the Mexican heartland. Only a tiny
parking lot and it does get crowded on weekends.

**New Hellas.** Monroe at Beaubien. (313) 961-5544.
The cognoscenti's choice in Greektown. Moussaka, lamb
in all its variations, sea bass, flaming cheese appetizers
(universally referred to as "opa") all washed down with a
cold glass of retsina. No wonder Detroiters flock to these
brightly lit blocks on the east side of downtown.

**Traffic Jam & Snug.** Second at Canfield.
(313) 831-9470. A Wayne State University hangout that
began life as a vegetarian restaurant and has since expanded to a full service menu of eclectic stuff. Great assortment
of cheeses, sandwiches, soups and some notable baked
goods at dessert time.

**Pizza Papalis.** 553 Monroe, in Greektown.
(313) 961-8020. Best pizza in the downtown area. Massive
slabs of stuffed Chicago-style deep dish pizza. Expanded
into an area-wide chain from this original location.

**Miller's Bar.** 23700 Michigan, Dearborn.
(313) 565-2577. Best burger around. Simple, unadorned, if
you want to order something else you're in the wrong
place. It's a bar but lots of families eat here. So do Ford
employees from the nearby headquarters.

**Cadieux Café.** Detroit. Cadieux north of Mack, on the east side, just a few blocks from Grosse Pointe.
(313) 882-8560. Mussels, Belgian beer and feather bowling in the side room. People trek from all over the area to taste these little mollusks in mustard sauce and wash it down with some of the best beer brewed.

# CITY WALKS

### *Strolling down Woodward*

The best way to get oriented in the city's compact downtown is to ride the **People Mover.** This elevated monorail encircles the area and gives you a pigeon's eye view, with vistas across the river into Canada as a bonus.

But it's sort of a low-rent theme park ride, constantly undergoing some sort of repairs and used heavily only during special events. There is no substitute for getting out and walking.

Since downtown is probably the safest and best-policed area of the city there is no need for trepidation.

Best place to start is **Grand Circus Park.** When Judge Augustus Woodward redrew the map of Detroit after a devastating fire in 1805, he designed a fan-shaped arrangement, with this park as its hub. Streets radiate out from it in eight directions with Woodward slicing through the center. (The judge modestly claimed that the street was not named for him but because it headed toward the woods. Whatever.)

The park, neglected for years, has once again become Grand because of the city's new stadiums and the revival of the theater district, all of which lies within a block or two.

Stand at Woodward and West Adams, at the northern edge of the park. Just to the north, on the west side of Woodward, are two great movie houses that were saved from demolition.

The nearest one is the State (once known as the Palms) which is used primarily for rock concerts and other live music events. On the next block is the **Fox**, which hosts road show musical extravaganzas.

*All aglow for a really big show*

The **Fox** is especially impressive, a 5,000 seat palace with an architectural style that can best be described as Persian-Indian-Burmese and Points East. It opened in 1928 and was the crowning achievement of theater architect, C. Howard Crane, who built many of Detroit's grand movie houses.

There are no regular tours, but see if you can get a peek at the lobby, which will give you some idea. Or better yet ante up and get a ticket for an event. The Fox, owned by the Ilitch family, who also owns the Detroit Tigers and Red Wings, regularly has topped the nation in gross ticket revenues since its restoration and reopening in 1988.

Right across Woodward is **Comerica Park,** with its carved tigers guarding the main entranceway. Inaugurated in 2000, the park's open feel, views of the downtown skyline and historical exhibits honoring the team's great players and moments, have won acceptance from baseball

*A beautiful skyline view at Comerica Park*

fans---even those who mourned the loss of Tiger Stadium, about one mile west of here.

Just beyond the ballpark, you can see the outline of **Ford Field,** the indoor stadium of the Detroit Lions, which opened in 2002. The critical mass of these two stadiums, with a combined seating capacity of over 100,000, has given a jolt of life to this area of downtown.

Now turn around. The statue of the seated gentleman right before you in the park is **Hazen Pingree,** the city's mayor in the 1890s. He won the eternal gratitude of its citizens by breaking up the streetcar monopoly and fighting for lower fares.

Two office towers flank the southern end of the park. On the right is the **David Whitney Building,** once the most prestigious address for area physicians. On the left is the **Broderick Tower.** Plans to turn these structures into a hotel and condos, respectively, have been on hold for several years. This being Detroit, almost anything can yet happen.

Across Broadway from the Broderick Tower is the **Detroit Opera House.** This is another converted movie theater (the Broadway Capitol) that has been successfully restored as a home for the Michigan Opera Company and other traveling shows.

Woodward narrows beyond the south end of **Grand**

**Circus Park** and becomes a canyon, hemmed in between the high Victorian facades of formerly fashionable stores. This was once the heart of the city's retail district. Renamed Merchants Row, many of these buildings are being converted to lofts, as Detroit tries to establish a residential base in the downtown area. These blocks are one of the city's great historical treasures, a potential base for a retail revival at the city's core.

The reason why becomes visible on the left, once you cross Gratiot Ave. This was once the location of the J.L. Hudson department store, which was second in square footage only to Macy's in New York's Herald Square as late as the 1950s. But as shopping patterns and ownership changed, the store shut down in 1983 and was imploded 15 years later.

In 2003, the site became the new headquarters for **Compuware.** This stunning glass structure, with a fountain-dappled atrium lobby, is the most significant sign of progress downtown in the last two decades. The software company was started up in the suburbs and, in an almost unprecedented move, its president, Peter Karmanos, decided to move downtown. There is a **Hard Rock Café,** a major bookstore and several smaller retail outlets inside. The hope is that the ripple effect will also bring some business back to the adjoining part of Woodward.

Cross the street and you're at the new **Campus Martius Place** and **Cadillac Square.** For most of the last 200 years, this vast open area was the central gathering place for the city; a site for political rallies and celebrations. In recent decades, that focus shifted a few blocks south to the riverfront. But it has returned to prominence with the opening of the adjacent Compuware Building and the redevelopment of Campus Martius. This urban park, which opened late in 2004, includes an ice skating rink, fountain and lots of benches to sit upon and take in the scene as it flows past.

The **Soldiers and Sailors Monument,** just to its south, in Cadillac Square, was erected right after the Civil War. According to legend, one of the figures depicted on it was modeled after the famous female abolitionist Sojourner

Truth. She was a frequent visitor to Detroit, although there is no proof that she actually sat for sculptor Randolph Rogers. Nevertheless, one of the city's first civil rights marches ended here in 1942 and a wreath dedicated to her memory was placed at the monument base.

Cross to the west side of Woodward, and on the next block you will see the **Guardian Building.** It's the one with the orange bricks, a shade that became known as "Guardian" because of the specifications for this structure.

Only New York and Chicago built more skyscrapers than Detroit in the 1920s and this one may be the most gracious of them all. The Guardian opened its doors in 1929 as the home of the city's largest real estate investment bank, the Guardian Detroit Union Group. Within three years, the Depression had killed it off. But its 40-story office building lives on.

Step into the lobby, magnificently decorated with terra cotta tile made in Detroit by the Pewabic Pottery. The red marble came from a Tunisian quarry that was specially reopened for the purpose. The ceiling frescoes were hand-painted and the vaulted lobby was modeled after the nave of Beauvais Cathedral in France. It was, in fact, hailed as a "Cathedral of Finance" by its planners.

The building was brilliantly restored by later occupants and now houses offices of the public utility, MichCon, as well as SHG (formerly Smith, Hinchman& Grylls), the architectural firm that originally designed it.

Just down the block is **One Woodward Avenue,** the work of Minoru Yamasaki, another nationally known architect who worked in the Detroit area. Completed in 1963, the white structure almost seems to float above the street, so gracefully does it ascend.

The building was also the site of one of the most famous practical jokes in the city's history. Right across Woodward is city hall, now named for Detroit's mayor of 20 years, the late Coleman A.Young. In front of that building is a huge Marshall Frederick sculpture, the **Spirit of Detroit.** But ever since its 1957 unveiling it has been referred to as the **Jolly Green Giant.**

A statue of an attractive **Indian maiden** stands in front of One Woodward Avenue. One wintry evening in the mid 60s, someone tracked giant footprints in the snow, leading from the Giant right across Woodward to the maiden. No one ever confessed to the scandalous prank.

On the far side of Jefferson Avenue, you can also see the **Big Fist,** a tribute to Joe Louis described in the Local Color section. The work, by sculptor Robert Graham, was the result of a cash grant to the **Detroit Institute of Arts** by *Sports Illustrated* magazine in 1986. It still raises some hackles among those who believe it represents black power. As recently as 2003 it was daubed with whitewash by some indignant suburban residents. But familiarity has bred acceptance.

*Convention facilities at Cobo Center*

Extending down to the river from this point is **Hart Plaza.** This area has replaced Cadillac Square as the city's official gathering place. When a Detroit sports team wins a championship, for example, this is where the celebration is held. It is also prime ground for outdoor concerts and people-watching.

Its most notable feature is the **Dodge Fountain,** a gift to the city from the auto-making family and a pleasant oasis on a hot summer day. **Cobo Center,** named for another former mayor, is on the right edge of the Plaza as you face the river, and beside it is the **Veterans Memorial.** This building (now known as the UAW Training Center) was opened in 1950, at approximately the same place Cadillac first came ashore 249 years before. It was the first element in the remaking of the waterfront, previously a warren of warehouses and docks. The 30-foot high eagle in front of it was the work of Fredericks, the same artist who rendered the Jolly Green Giant.

Walk up to the railing and take in the river scene. Wait for one of the huge **Great Lakes freighters** to pass by, a magical sight as its massive bulk slips silently past the city. On weekends, the area is dotted with pleasure craft; sailing out from marinas on the American side of this international waterway and from Windsor, the Canadian city across the way.

It's a good place to gather energy for the second half of this walk.

### East Side of Downtown

At the eastern extremity of **Hart Plaza,** which is named for Michigan's late U.S. Senator Philip Hart, rise the cylindrical glass towers of the **Renaissance Center.** Built under the leadership of Henry Ford II, it is now world headquarters of General Motors.

The place is filled with such ironies. It stands beside the city's most attractive asset, the river, but when it opened, there was no place from which to see the water. GM has corrected the error and built a **Winter Garden** on its river side. Intended as a new beginning for downtown, it walled itself off from the old downtown behind massive berms, giving the place the look of a fortress. The berms were finally removed in 2004. Attempting to spark a retail revival, it ended up confusing shoppers with its circular layout. They couldn't find the stores they were looking for, wandered around in frustration and finally all the stores moved out.

It is certainly not a failure, but it never fulfilled the promise claimed for it at its 1977 opening. Nevertheless, architect John Portman's design has become the visual symbol of Detroit.

On the way, however, take note of the little Anglican church that huddles in the RenCen's massive shadow. **Mariners Church,** built in 1842, is the oldest stone house of worship in the city. The interior is filled with nautical imagery, following the stipulation of the two sisters who founded it as a memorial for Great Lakes sailors.

Those who know Gordon Lightfoot's song, **"The Wreck of the Edmund Fitzgerald,"** know that the bell of this church is tolled whenever a mariner is lost on the Lakes.

Enter the RenCen from the Jefferson entrance for a look around. The signage has improved since GM took over, with color coding and improved access to the second level. But this place can still be a trap for the unwary. With exterior lines of sight cut off, 5.5 million square feet of space and a floor plan laid out in concentric circles, it can get more than a bit confusing.

The observation deck on the 72nd floor is now open to the public. The space is occupied by a new restaurant, **Coach Insignia,** opened in 2004. In the original design this restaurant revolved, but diners now must be content with a stationary view of the city. That view, which takes in most of southeastern Michigan and Canada, from Lake Erie to Lake St. Clair, is spectacular.

Here's a tip. If you don't want to order a meal (although the food is quite good), you can head to the bar and take in the scenery for the price of a drink or a pop. But if you're in shorts and a tank top, you'll probably be turned away at the security elevator on the ground floor.

There are a few things to see at street level. GM World, on Level A, shows off the new vehicles of the auto-making giant, with interactive displays and exhibits on the corporation's history and global reach. GM also uses it for special events, so it's best to call first to see if it is open. The number is (313) 667-7151. Otherwise, it is open Monday to Friday, 9 a.m. to 9 p.m., free.

You should also make your way around to the south side of the complex to the **Winter Garden** for an up-close view of the **Detroit River** and **Canada** in a spectacular glassed-in setting. (Yes, that's a southern exposure. This is the only place in the United States where our northern neighbor is actually situated to the south.) There are also shops along the path, including some upscale clothing stores, as the **RenCen** makes another try at going retail.

Once you complete the circuit of the towers, leave the RenCen from the north side, cross Jefferson Avenue and walk straight ahead on Brush Street. The **Millender Center,** an office-hotel complex will be on the left, and the Bricktown area on the right. There are some interesting restaurants and bars there. One of the most venerable is **Jacoby's,** which began life in 1904 as a German beer garden and still serves up the suds. It remains a popular gathering place for attorneys and politicians.

At Monroe Street, turn right and you will be entering **Greektown.** This is downtown's liveliest strip, an ongoing party of predominantly Aegean-style cuisine, with a little Irish, Cajun and Italian thrown in, too. On warm summer nights, the crowds line up in front of the most popular restaurants until very late. The entrance to the **Greektown Casino** is also here.

Take notice of the **Second Baptist Church,** at 441 Monroe, the oldest black congregation in the city and a leading station on the Underground Railroad.

At Beaubien, take a left. Many of the streets in this part of the city have French names, reminders of 18th Century landowners. They laid out their property in ribbon farms, narrow strips that ran for miles into the interior. These streets follow the course of the old farms. Turn left at Macomb and then a right back on Brush. (This intersection is the source of one of the oldest schoolboy jokes in the city. **Macomb and Brush.** Say the names real fast.) Across Gratiot, you'll see the **Hilton Garden Hotel,** the newest in downtown, opening in 2004, and an excellent base for attending sports events and the theater.

Right behind the hotel is **Harmonie Park,** a triangular-shaped oasis with a constantly changing assortment of restaurants, boutiques and galleries. The **Hunter House** is an excellent choice for a burger stop. The park is named for a 19th Century German social club, the Harmonie, which still occupies its northern end.

Keep walking through the park, along Grand River to Madison. On the other side of the street are the **Gem** and **Century Theaters.** They are housed in a building that was put on wheeled hoists and moved here from several blocks away, out of the way of the new baseball stadium. At the time, it was the largest building ever moved such a distance. The Century Club serves dinner for those attending performances.

Just to the right, at Brush, is the **Music Hall.** These three smaller houses mount revues and more intimate shows, and are part of the reason Detroit claims to have the highest concentration of live theater in its downtown than anywhere else in America but Times Square.

Turn left on Madison, past the **Detroit Athletic Club,** another of Albert Kahn's masterful buildings. If you then turn right on John R you will be alongside **Comerica Park,** with a good view of the ballpark's interior.

Turn left on Adams, and in one block you'll be back at **Grand Circus Park** and the starting point of these walks through downtown.

# A CITY DRIVE

Detroit has some wonderful historic neighborhoods if you know where to look. This little drive will take you to four of the most appealing---Corktown, Woodbridge, New Center Commons and Boston-Edison.

From a downtown base, head west on Michigan Avenue. As soon as you cross the bridge over the Lodge Freeway (U.S. 10), make a left on Brooklyn and then an immediate right on Leverette. This will place you in the midst of **Corktown.**

The area bills itself as Detroit's oldest neighborhood. Many of the frame homes here date from the Civil War era, a rare historic grouping in a city that grew too quickly to preserve much of its past. Several of these houses were renovated by young families who work downtown, which is within easy walking distance, or by those who like the feel of an historic area. As the name indicates, it was once the city's Irish neighborhood.

That large high-rise looming off to the left, incidentally, is what remains of the **Michigan Central Depot.** Once Detroit's grand railroad terminal, it has been deserted for years and probably has the world's largest collection of broken windows. Filmmakers are fond of using it as a symbol of urban decay.

At the end of Leverette, turn right on Rosa Parks Blvd. (The street sign may also say 12th Street, but it was officially renamed for the civil rights heroine, a Detroit resident, several years ago.)

Follow this street past Grand River, take a quick right onto Willis and then a left on Avery. Now you are in Woodbridge, one of Detroit's most fashionable addresses between 1890 and 1910. Many bankers lived here and so did baseball great Ty Cobb.

Many of the homes have been lovingly restored by those who enjoy the proximity of downtown. Some of them have been painted in pastel shades, giving a cheerful tone to the area. Others, however, remain in a state of semi-dilapidation. It is still among the city's most atmospheric areas.

At Warren, turn right and then, once back across the Lodge, watch for Third Avenue and make a left. This divided thoroughfare will take you through the middle of the **Wayne State University** campus, with classroom buildings on either side. You may want to return there when you visit the museums of the **Cultural Center.**

At the northern edge of the university, the road swings to the right and becomes Second Avenue. Soon you will see the **Fisher Building** rising straight ahead. This Albert Kahn designed skyscraper is the core of the **New Center** area and a good place to get out for a short walk.

The building is one of America's Art Deco masterpieces. It was built by the Fisher Brothers, who designed the first enclosed automobile chassis and got rich making them for General Motors. The Fisher Building was intended to be their showcase. The 28-story tower seems higher than it actually is because of the dramatic use of setbacks and shadows. But it is the interior of this skyscraper that is the big show.

The Fishers insisted that every square inch of the lobby be adorned with rare marbles and mosaics. They got their wish. A more ornate space in a commercial structure is hard to imagine.

Detroit's largest legitimate theater, also named the **Fisher,** has been located here since 1961, replacing an earlier movie house from the 1920s. During the Christmas season, the lobby is one of the most festive places in the entire city, with ornamented trees and decorations everywhere.

From the building's southern entrance, across West Grand Boulevard, is the former **General Motors Building.** This powerful structure, intended by Kahn to symbolize the industrial might of its original occupants, now houses State offices and has been renamed Cadillac Place. Opened in 1923, the long, solid row of columns on the building's façade is the grounded antithesis of the soaring Fisher Building.

From the far end of the Fisher Building lobby, walk up Second one block to Pallister Street and turn left. This is the most fully realized portion of a revitalization plan for the New Center area, initiated by GM in the 1980s. Pallister is closed to motorized traffic for this one block. The homes, most of them dating from the 1890s, have been restored and antique street lamps installed. Walking down this street it is easy to recapture a sense of what Detroit must have looked like before the automobile altered everything.

Return to your car and continue driving north on Second for one mile. Just across Clairmont, you'll enter the **Boston-Edison Historic District,** the largest in the city and one of the largest in the country.

When the big money came pouring into Detroit in the 20th Century's second decade, this is what it built. These spacious homes, in a variety of styles that range from English Manor to Spanish Colonial, reflect the eclectic tastes and individuality of their builders. These were people making a strong statement about their status. No cookie-cutter design for them. Each one was unique unto itself.

There are five east-west streets in the district and it is eight blocks wide, from Woodward on the east to Linwood on the west. The best drive is west along Chicago Blvd., since it has the only bridge across the freeway. If you want to duck down Boston Blvd., however, you may note that on the northeast corner of Hamilton is the stately home built by the **Kresge** family (the business which later became K-Mart). It was later occupied by Berry Gordy, of Motown Records.

The best route back downtown is to make your way over to Woodward and take a right. It's a direct shot, and on the way you'll pass through the midst of the Cultural Center. This is an area you'll want to return to on foot to explore its four major museums.

## ALONG THE RIVER TO LAKE ST. CLAIR

It was during Thomas Jefferson's presidency that Detroit's road system was laid out, so it is only right that one of the city's primary avenues should bear his name. East Jefferson parallels the course of the Detroit River. After entering the Grosse Pointes, its name changes to Lake Shore Road as it runs beside Lake St. Clair. Pick up East Jefferson on the north side of the Renaissance Center and start heading east.

Detroit is redeveloping its waterfront in this area. It used to be an unappealing tangle of railroad tracks, warehouses and a few industrial plants. Now parks and new developments are starting to make inroads.

Turn right on Orleans and follow it to Atwater, the street nearest the river, then turn left. The **Tri-Centennial State Park and Marina** is a good example of what's been done here. Plans eventually call for a continuous line of parks and walk-

*The Ren Cen rises along the Detroit River*

ways between here and the Belle Isle Bridge, about a mile to the east. The unsightly smokestacks of old cement plants block the way, however, and the problem of relocating these companies has yet to be resolved. But the park, with the towers of the RenCen rising just behind it, is a vision of what may come.

Continue along Atwater and in a few blocks you'll reach **River Place**, a development formed from the campus of Parke-Davis. The historic brick buildings of the former pharmaceutical maker have been adapted to other uses and there is also a pleasant walkway along the water here.

Take Joseph Campau back to Jefferson and turn right. In a few blocks, you'll see the sign to the **Belle Isle Bridge.** This crossing leads to the city's island park, a 1,000 acre gem in the midst of the Detroit River.

Upkeep has been a problem for the constantly cash-strapped city and there are a few blemishes here. But Belle Isle remains Detroit's breath of fresh air and its primary recreation ground. There are beaches, canals, athletic fields for softball, even a Sunday morning cricket pitch.

Turn right from the bridge and follow the road that makes a counter-clockwise circuit of the island. There are outstanding views of the city skyline from the island's western end, and as the road swings along the south shore you'll see vistas of Canada and the traffic on the river.

You will also see signs for the island's three museums: The **Whitcomb Conservatory, Aquarium** (closed) and **Dossin Great Lakes Museum.** Descriptions of these facilities and their opening hours can be found in the Museum section of the book.

Keep following the road as it cuts back across the center of the island and then returns to the bridge (formally named in honor of Gen. Douglas MacArthur). Once back on the mainland, turn right on Jefferson and continue east.

In a few blocks is another of the city's most evocative neighborhoods, **Indian Village.** Only three blocks wide, it is lined with homes built by the city's elite in the 1890s and is designated an historic district.

To get a quick look at what's here, turn left on Seminole, follow it up to Charlevoix, then right and another right on Iroquois to return to East Jefferson.

The city's most extensive group of luxury apartments and condos now line up along the river side of Jefferson. You'll also pass **Waterworks Park,** a facility that has been closed since 1941 when civic officials feared that America's enemies planned to poison the water supply. At Conner, you'll pass the massive **Chrysler Plant,** one of the few remaining automobile factories within the city itself.

Continue east and in another mile you'll cross into **Grosse Pointe Park.** The change in ambience is immediately apparent; from an especially rundown portion of the city to one of its finest suburbs. It has been pointed out repeatedly that the street defining this border is named Alter Road.

You will see the stately homes of the **Pointes** down each side street as you proceed deeper into high rent territory. Most of the mansions of the old automotive tycoons are gone. They were too expensive to maintain and the property was far more lucrative as the site of several smaller homes.

Each of the communities maintains a private park for its residents. Unless you become pals with someone who lives here, you won't be allowed to enter. But just as the road enters **Grosse Pointe Farms** and reaches the edge of Lake St. Clair is the **War Memorial.** This is a public facility where you can park and walk around for a look at the gardens and the water.

From here on, Lake Shore is a divided highway with wonderfully tranquil views across the water. **St. Clair** is not included among the Great Lakes, although it does encompass 460 square miles. There are periodic attempts in Congress to classify it as a Great Lake to obtain federal funds. But it's still a pretty good lake, and the number of boats that sail and roar across its waters on any summer weekend is a good indicator of its place in the hearts of this community.

You can follow Lake Shore all the way up to the Macomb County line. But the best way back to downtown is to take a left at Vernier Road, right at the Grosse Pointe Yacht Club, and take that to westbound I-94 (the Ford Freeway). Then turn on southbound I-75 and 375, which empties onto East Jefferson in the shadow of the RenCen.

### *Boat Trips*

Diamond Jack's River Tours. (313) 843-7676. This 125-passenger boat started off as a ferry in northern Michigan, running between Charlevoix and Beaver Island in Lake Michigan and then as part of the service to Mackinac Island. It has been used for Detroit River tours since 1991.

The two-hour trips runs from May to October. Sailings are scheduled at 1 p.m. and 3:30 p.m., Thursday to Sunday. Fare is $14 for adults, $10 under 16, $12 for seniors and 5 and under free. There are no advance reservations and no credit cards are accepted. Special packages are available.

The boat takes in all the major sights along the waterway, between its two outlets at Lake Erie and Lake St. Clair. It may be boarded either in downtown Detroit or in Wyandotte. The Detroit dock is at the eastern edge of Hart Plaza, at the foot of Bates Street, immediately west of the RenCen. In Wyandotte it leaves from Bishop Park, at the foot of Superior Street, off Biddle.

### *Fishing Charter*

Best bet in arranging an expedition for walleye in Lake Erie is Bray's Charters. This Detroit-based company, owned by Capt. Tommy Bray, will also take anglers through the Detroit River and Lake St. Clair on its 27-foot Thompson craft, *Popular Hill*. Call (313) 273-9183. Season is April through October.

# SHOPPING

As indicated previously, there is no significant retail presence in downtown Detroit. Aside from a limited number of stores in office buildings--the RenCen, Compuware headquarters, the Fisher Building--you have to look elsewhere for shopping opportunities.

You will find them across the river in Windsor, at major malls in Dearborn and Livonia, in downtown districts in Grosse Pointe and Plymouth and a few other places.

**Windsor.** Ouellette (pronounce it "wol-let" and you'll be reasonably close) is the main street. There are little shops all along its length, for seven or eight blocks south from the riverfront. You'll find good buys here on Canadian-made products, clothing, china and cigars---although the Cuban variety cannot be legally imported into the United States.

**Lazare's Furs and Leathers,** at 493 Ouellette, is noted for high-end products in those lines. A short cab ride away is one of the best clothing stores in Ontario, Freed's, with some incredible bargains on men's suits. It's at 1526 Ottawa Street. If you are driving from downtown, take Wyandotte Street east, then north on Gladstone St. to Ottawa. It should take about five minutes.

Purchases are subject to the usual duty-free exclusions for foreign travel. If you want to stop at the duty-free shop on the Canadian side of the border crossing, you can get a refund on local taxes. That is also a good place to look for bargains in liquor.

Windsor is connected to Detroit by the Ambassador Bridge and the Detroit-Windsor Tunnel. The tunnel, which runs between the two downtowns, is the far more convenient method. The entrance is immediately west of the RenCen, off East Jefferson, and it emerges in Canada one-half block east of Ouellette. Just make a left after you go through Canadian customs and you're there.

If you want to do it by bus, your hotel will have the latest information on schedules and pickup points. Or you can call Transit Windsor at (519) 944-4111.

This border crossing has tightened up considerably since 9/11. You will be asked for a passport. This is the busiest crossing point in North America and there are times when it jams up with absolutely no advance warning. Weekend evenings and late Sunday afternoon are especially dicey.

If you do go to Windsor be sure to walk to the parks on the river at the foot of Ouellette for postcard views of the Detroit skyline.

**Grosse Pointe.** There are two distinct shopping areas here: the **Hill** and the **Village**. Both are located on Kercheval Street, two long blocks north of Jefferson Avenue.

The **Village** is in Grosse Pointe City, just east of Cadieux, while the **Hill**, is about one mile away, just east of Fisher Road, in Grosse Pointe Farms.

Don't come looking for funky. These are conservative communities and the apparel stores here reflect that taste, with an affluent spin. They are both pleasant walking areas, however, and give a nice insight into these tradition-bound towns.

**Dearborn.** Fairlane Town Center. A mall of significant size, with about 180 shops, anchored by Lord & Taylor, Marshall Field's and Penney's. It is a short walk from the Hyatt Regency Hotel, in the vicinity of Ford World

Headquarters, on Michigan Avenue at the Southfield Freeway. There are also movie theaters here.

**Dearborn.** West Warren Avenue. The Detroit area is home to the largest Arab-American community in the country. By some estimates it numbers 250,000 people, and the largest concentration is in Dearborn. There is more than a little irony in this development, in view of the fact that Orville Hubbard, its longtime mayor, prided himself in keeping non-white, non-Christians out of his town. But times change, and these new citizens, mostly from Lebanon and Syria, have transformed this part of Dearborn into a fascinating slice of Middle Eastern culture.

The center of the Warren Avenue shopping strip runs between Meyers Road, on the east, to Chase Street. You'll find restaurants, souvenir shops, bakeries. Most of the stores have signs written in both English and Arabic and feature food that is halal---acceptable to Muslim dietary laws. There is even a little strip mall at Warren and Chase.

Easiest way to get here from downtown is to take U.S. 10 (Lodge Freeway) north to westbound I-94, and then on to the Ford Road exit. Make a quick right on Wyoming Avenue, then left in about one mile on Warren. The district begins one-half mile west of this point.

**Livonia. Laurel Park Place.** A smaller, more manageable sort of mall with the Parisian and Von Maur as the anchor stores. Several of the shops here are one-of-a-kind in this area. It is connected to the Livonia Marriott Hotel. There are also movies here. It's located at I-275 and Six Mile Road.

**Hamtramck.** Another ethnic experience, this one predominantly Polish. The corner of Joseph Campau and Caniff is the center of things, with little stores, bakeries and knick knack shops branching off from there. This once was a center of Polish immigration, although the town is only about one-third its former size. It also has developed a rather sizable Muslim community, which is predominantly

Albanian. Still, many former residents make sentimental journeys back for holiday shopping and church services.

**The Polish Art Center,** at 9539 Joseph Campau, is the perfect place for picking up crafts and artwork straight from Europe. Take I-75 (Chrysler Freeway) north from downtown to Caniff and then right to Joseph Campau.

**Plymouth.** Its downtown is built around a little park, a setting that resembles small town New England. Side streets filled with shops and galleries branch off from Main and Ann Arbor Trail, the central intersection. Restaurants and coffee houses add to the ambience. The perfect place for purposeful browsing.

Take I-96 (Jeffries Freeway) west from downtown. Once past the I-275 intersection the highway will become M-14. Exit at Sheldon Road and take a left. Then left again at Ann Arbor Trail to reach downtown.

**Detroit.** There are a few bright spots for shopping in Detroit. The Broadway-Randolph area, on the east side of downtown, has several clothing stores, most of them catering to an urban clientele. The **Broadway,** at 1247 Broadway, and Serman's, at 1238 Randolph, both fit into this category and feature name-brand attire.

Another local institution is **Hot Sam's,** at Brush and Macomb. It got its distinct nickname in the 1960s when young men were especially impressed with the cutting edge styles stocked here.

**Henry the Hatter** is one of the most venerable downtown stores, dating back to the late 19th Century. Although it origi-nated at a time when no well-dressed male would leave the house without a hat, it is still going strong when hats are regarded as a statement rather than a necessity. There is a downtown store at 1307 Broadway, and a branch in Hamtramck, in the Joseph Campau-Caniff shopping district.

For book-lovers, the **John K. King** store is a needful stop. It specializes in used and hard-to-find books, logically categorized over three floors of open stacks. There is also on-site parking. It is located at 901 W. Lafayette, just east of the Lodge Freeway Service Drive.

For those interested in African-American material, the **Shrine of the Black Madonna** claims the largest selection of such books in the country. There are also art and gifts from Africa on sale. It is located at 13535 Livernois. That is about a 15-minute drive from downtown by way of the Lodge Freeway, then left at the Livernois exit.

**Dumouchelles Art Galleries** has the broadest range of art objects and antiques in the city and its monthly auctions always draw a large, knowledgeable crowd. It is right across the street from the RenCen, at 409 E. Jefferson.

**Pure Detroit,** in the **RenCen,** is the best bet for memorabilia of the city. Tee-shirts, books of local interest, made-in-Detroit products. There are other locations in the Guardian and Fisher buildings.

**Eastern Market.** This is one of the city's genuine jewels, a traditional farmer's market on steroids. Growers from Michigan, Ohio and Ontario truck in their produce and set up at the sheds. There are also fixed-site stores selling every kind of food under the sun---from peanuts to pork. There are more than a dozen restaurants in the mix, as well as antique stores. The market has been located here since 1841 and draws big crowds on Saturday mornings when entire families come. It opens at 7 a.m. every day but Sunday.

The market is just east of downtown, but a bit too far for a leisurely walk. Best bet is to cab it. If you're driving, leave downtown on Gratiot Avenue and just after crossing the I-375 bridge, turn left on Russell Street. This will lead you right into the heart of the market. Best walking streets there are Russell and Riopelle, one block to the east.

# MUSEUMS

*Choose your ride at Greenfield Village*

The **Henry Ford.** 20900 Oakwood Blvd. Dearborn. Monday to Saturday, 9:30 a.m. to 5 p.m.; Sunday opening at noon. Adult admission is $14, $9 for ages 5-12, free for 4 and under, for the Henry Ford Museum, and $20 for adults, $14 for ages 5-12 and free for 4 and under, for **Greenfield Village.** (313) 271-1620. Its hours are 9:30-5:00 every day from April to October, and 9:30-5:00 Friday to Sunday, November to December. Take I-96 west from the downtown area to southbound M-39 (Southfield Freeway). Exit at Oakwood and turn right into the museum complex.

The Henery Ford is one of America's greatest museums, worth a journey in itself. This institution was founded by the automaker in 1929. He meant it as a tribute to his great friend, Thomas A. Edison; a preservation of the world the two men had changed forever.

The two museums take their look back from different perspectives. The Henry Ford Museum is situated indoors.

In its eight-acre central hall, 200 years of industrial

progress are lined up for review. The history of every con-
ceivable machine that plays a part in our lives---from vacu-
um cleaners to stoves to radios---is traced from their primi-
tive beginnings to the sleek marvels of today.

The automotive section is excellent, as you might expect,
and there are exhibits on how cars changed the texture of the
American road. There are also sections on decorative arts and
historic curiosities---the chair Lincoln sat in when he was
assassinated, the bus on which Rosa Parks refused to move to
the back.

**Greenfield Village** is the outdoor portion of the com-
plex, named for the crossroads where Ford grew up after the
Civil War, just a few miles from here. Historic structures have
been assembled from all over the country. The Wright
Brothers cycle shop from Dayton, Ohio. Noah Webster's house
from New Haven, Ct.  Edison's lab from West Orange, N.J.
There is also a London jeweler's shop and a cottage from the
English Cotswolds.

They are set up as an idealized village. Stephen Foster
writes his songs over here, while Luther Burbank conducts
his horticultural experiments over there. Ford's first assembly plant in Detroit also is reproduced. Historic stores, inns
and churches complete the setting, as riverboats, horses-
and-buggies and antique cars make a circuit of the grounds.

If you have to choose just one, the Village may be the
better bet for young children. But this is an attraction
worth a few days; certainly as much as you'd give to a
theme park.

There is also the **Benson Ford Research Center,**
(313) 982-6020, open 9-5 Monday through Friday, and it is
free. A superb IMAX theatre, (313) 982-6001, with prices
ranging from $8.50-$11.75.

The Henry Ford Museum is also starting point for trips through the Rouge Plant. Reopened in 2004 after a 24-year hiatus, this tour is an unforgettable look at the inner workings of one of America's basic industries.

Even those who have seen an assembly line before will marvel at the finely calibrated movements that transform hunks of metal and glass into the newest vehicles on the market. You are looking at the true soul of Detroit, the rhythm of the city.

The tours include a film introduction and a walk of about one-third of a mile through the production facility. Advance tickets are a must. Call (313) 982-6001 for a reservation at a specific time. Adult prices are $14; children ages 3-12 are $10 and under 3 are free.

**Henry Ford Estate.** Dearborn. 4901 Evergreen Road, on the campus of the University of Michigan-Dearborn. Tours are given Monday to Saturday, April through December and 10 and 11 a.m. and 1, 2 and 3 p.m. Monday to Friday, January through March, 1:30 p.m. to 4:30 p.m. Sundays, all year, every half hour from 1 p.m. to 4:30 p.m. (313) 593-5590. Admission $10; ages 5 to 12, $6; and less than 5 are free.

While you're in the neighborhood, drop in on **Fair Lane**, the Ford estate, situated on a more bucolic stretch of the Rouge River. As you may have noticed, the estate also gave its name to the nearby shopping mall, Fairlane Town Center, which occupies land once owned by Ford.

It is a surprisingly modest home when compared to the mansions of other auto magnates, considering that its owner once was believed to be the richest man in the world. Sure, it has 56 rooms. But the sumptuous décor and art that characterized so many other stately homes is either lacking or downplayed.

What is fascinating are the personal items owned by Ford and his wife, Clara, and the magnificent gardens surrounding the house, which dates from 1915.

*Trucks rolling off the assembly line*

**Edsel and Eleanor Ford House.** 1100 Lake Shore Road, Grosse Pointe Shores. Tuesday to Saturday, 10 a.m. to 4 p.m., and Sunday, noon to 4 p.m.; April through December. Tuesday to Sunday, noon to 4 p.m., rest of year. (313) 884-4222. Admission $7; under 12, $5; under 5, free.

Now this is more like it. This is as much a museum as a house, a rambling mansion on Lake St. Clair fit for a member of the English nobility.

Henry did not approve of his son Edsel's taste for the finer things. He remained an engineer until the end of his life, while Edsel was fascinated by stylish, beautiful cars. The Lincoln was his baby.

Henry frequently belittled his son in front of company executives and fired his closest ally while Edsel was out of the country. While he bore the title of president, Edsel was never empowered to make major decisions. He died of a heart attack in 1943 at the age of 49. Most Ford commentators believe it was induced by stress from dad.

This house mirrors the taste and personality of Edsel and his wife. Their extensive collection of fine and decorative art was among the most admired in America. The 60-room home with its landscaped gardens running down to the water is a showplace in itself.

### Automotive Hall of Fame.

21400 Oakwood Blvd., Dearborn. Daily, 9 a.m. to 5 p.m., November through April. Closed Monday, rest of year.

(313) 240-4000. Admission $6; under 18, $3.

Located just down the road from the Henry Ford, this museum has exhibits on the other people who shaped the automotive industry, both in the United States and overseas. You'll see tributes to the founders of Chrysler, Porsche, Toyota, Ferrari, Chevrolet, and even failed geniuses such as Preston Tucker.

*Viewing automotive history*

### Motown Historical Museum.

2648 West Grand Blvd., Detroit. 10 a.m. to 6 p.m.,Tuesday to Saturday. Admission is $8 for adults, $5 for 12 and under. (313) 875-2264. Take the Lodge Freeway north from downtown. Exit at West Grand Blvd. and turn left for half a mile.

A musical miracle happened here (see Local Color). It was in this ordinary house that one of the defining sounds of American pop music was born. From 1959 to 1968, the artists of Motown came here to make the records that sent the sound of Detroit around the world.

The original studios are still in place. There is memorabilia and photographs of the stars who sang here and of the founder, Berry Gordy, Jr. The museum has become a place of pilgrimage especially for those who had their musical sensibilities shaped by the Motown Sound. There is also a gift shop.

**Pewabic Pottery.** 10125 East Jefferson, Detroit. 10 a.m. to 6 p.m., Monday to Saturday. Free. (313) 822-0954.

The glazed tiles created here since 1907 can be seen in public buildings all across the United States, and especially in the historic homes and skyscrapers of Detroit. Even Comerica Park, which opened in 2000, includes material from Pewabic as an authentic local touch.

The unique glow that marks Pewabic tiles was developed by Mary Chase Perry Stratton during the height of the Arts and Crafts Movement. This was a revolt against manufactured mediocrity, and was meant to restore the personal touch of the artisan. Pewabic's workshops have been bustling ever since and its studios are a National Historic Landmark.

You can observe the ceramics process in action here and visit the pottery's gallery, museum and gift shop.

**Cultural Center Museums.** These four facilities are located within an easy walk of each other, in the Woodward-Warren area, about two miles north of downtown.

**Detroit Institute of Arts,** 5200 Woodward Avenue. 10 a.m. to 4 p.m., Wednesday to Friday; open until 9 p.m., Saturday and Sunday 10 a.m. to 5 p.m. (313) 833-7900. Adult admission $4; ages 6-17, $1; under 6, free.

One of the nation's most prestigious art museums. Great Flemish and Italian Renaissance collections. The African art galleries were donated by the late Gov. G. Mennen Williams and the armor by newspaper tycoon William Randolph Hearst. But its most famous feature is the murals painted by Diego Rivera. Engaged to celebrate the achievements of American industry, the Mexican artist also included subtle reminders of his leftist political leanings. Outraged patrons threatened to close it down as Marxist propaganda, but the work is now a treasured part

*The Rivera Court at the Institute of Arts*

of the city's past.

The Institute also features first-rate traveling exhibits throughout the year.

**Detroit Historical Museum,** 5401 Woodward. 10 a.m. to 5 p.m., Tuesday to Saturday; Sunday opens at 11 a.m. (313) 833-1805. Admission $5; under 8, $3.

A very good overview of the city's history; from its founding as a French outpost, to its often violent years under British rule, to its rise as an industrial giant. The most popular exhibit is the Streets of Old Detroit, recreating thoroughfares from different periods in the city's history, with artifacts from businesses that actually existed at each time.

**Charles H. Wright Museum of African-American History,** 315 E. Warren Ave. Tuesday to Saturday, 9:30 a.m. to 5 p.m.; Sunday opens at 1 p.m, closes at 5:00 p.m.. (313) 494-5800. Admission $8; over 62 and under 13, $5.

The museum is named for the Detroit physician who labored for years to make the museum a reality; starting with displays in his own office and finally winning civic support for this striking facility. With the largest percentage of African-American residents of any large city in the United States, the museum is a special point of pride locally. It features excellent displays on slavery and the horrific middle passage, as well as belongings of prominent African-Americans, from astronauts to civil rights heroes.

*Dramatic exhibits abound at the Wright Museum*

**New Detroit Science Center,** 5020 John R. Tuesday-Friday, 9 a.m. to 5 p.m.; Saturday, 10:30 a.m. to 6 p.m., Sunday 12-6 p.m. (313) 577-8400. Admission $7, plus $4 to the IMAX movie theater.

A good stop for kids, with lots of hand-on science, a planetarium and the stunning IMAX Dome Theatre, showing movies that surround spectators with breath-taking visual images.

*The Detroit Science Center is fun for kids*

**Belle Isle Museums.** All of them are within a quarter-mile of each other near the southern end of the city park in the Detroit River. The island is described in the City Drives section and is accessible by bridge from East Jefferson Avenue at the foot of East Grand Boulevard.

**Anna Scripps Whitcomb Conservatory,** 7000 Inselruhe. Daily, 10 a.m. to 5 p.m. (313) 852-4065. Donation is asked.

The conservatory was built in 1904, designed by the famed architect, Albert Kahn. There is more than an acre of plant life under its glass roof, but the prime attraction is its orchid collection. It is the largest city-owned orchid display in the country and was a gift from the late Mrs. Whitcomb, in whose honor the name of the conservatory was changed.

**Belle Isle Aquarium,** adjacent to the Conservatory, at Inselruhe at Loiter Way. Closed in 2005 for an indefinite period.

**Dossin Great Lakes Museum,** 100 Strand Drive. Weekends, 11 a.m. to 5 p.m. Other times by appointment. (313) 852-4051. Donation asked.

The history of shipping on the Lakes, with a special section on power boat racing. Displays on historic vessels and momentous wrecks.

**Tuskegee Airmen National Museum.** On the grounds of Fort Wayne, at 6325 West Jefferson. 10 a.m. to 3 p.m., Tuesday to Sunday, April through September. (313) 843-8849. Donation asked.

The history and mementoes of this organization of black fighter pilots, who had to combat racism as well as the Axis during World War II, is preserved in this facility. The city's late mayor, Coleman A. Young, belonged to this group, which got its name from its training base at the famed Alabama institute.

It is located at Fort Wayne, the oldest surviving Civil War era fortification on the Great Lakes. It never fired a shot in anger but is regarded as a great example of military architecture of that period. The fort is open on summer weekends, 11 a.m. to 4 p.m.

**Ford Field.** 2000 Brush, Detroit. Tours are given at 11 a.m. and 1 p.m., Monday to Friday. Call for reservations. (313) 262-2000. Adults, $7; under 12, $5; under 5, free.

The home stadium of the Detroit Lions is among the finest facilities in the National Football League. It incorporates part of a former department store warehouse in its suites section, and although it is a dome, the huge exterior windows give it a bright, open feel. The tour includes everything on the premises from private suites to locker rooms.

# COUNTRY WALKS

The Detroit area sprawls in all directions from its downtown base, a movement fueled by a world-class freeway system. The **Huron-Clinton Metroparks,** however, have managed to preserve close-in patches of green for quiet getaways and encounters with the natural world.

Three of them are linked along the Huron River, just south of Detroit Metropolitan Airport. The Huron rises in the hills west of Ann Arbor, flows through the heart of that college town and nearby Ypsilanti, before running through this green belt on the way to its outlet in Lake Erie. The fourth of these Metroparks is situated right on the lake.

The three river parks, running north to south, are **Lower Huron, Willow** and **Oakwoods.** All of them have paved hiking-biking trails, which can be followed either in loops that run from 3 to 4.5 miles in length or through all three of the parks, a round trip of 30 miles.

**Lower Huron,** 1,258 acres, has a swimming pool with waterslide, self-guiding nature trail and ice-skating ponds in winter.

**Willow** features an Olympic-sized pool, skate park, cross country ski trails and a 17-acre nature pond. Single speed bikes can be rented here for $3 an hour, with a $10 deposit. Rowboats and paddleboats are available at the pond for $5 to $8 an hour.

**Oakwoods** is the best bet for hiking, with five miles of wooded trails right along the river. There is also a nature center that displays animals that inhabit the park and a birding center, which includes a woodcock watch. Fishing is allowed from rowboats or canoes and in a few areas from the river's banks.

All three parks can be reached by taking I-94 west from the city, just past the airport. For Lower Huron, exit at southbound Haggerty Road and follow the signs. For Willow, take I-94 to southbound I-275 and exit at South Huron. Then take an immediate left on Bell Road, and another left on Willow Road. For Oakwoods, continue on I-275 to eastbound Will Carleton Road.

The parks are open all year. The daily admission fee is $4 per vehicle and there is no overnight camping for individuals. (734) 697-9181.

**Lake Erie Metropark** stretches across three miles of lakeshore and is one of the great bird-watching areas on the Great Lakes. It is directly on the flight path of migrating hawks, and a festival celebrating these raptors is held in September. There is also an ongoing bird-watching walk program at the park's nature center.

Although it is on the lake, there are no beaches here. The shoreline is mostly marsh and rock. There is, however, a wave pool. There are no boat rental facilities, either, but there is a launch site, giving access to the lake's rich store of walleye. A permit is required.

From downtown Detroit, take southbound I-75 to the Huron River Drive exit, then east to the park entrance. The park is open all year. Call (734) 379-5020.

# GOLF

The **Rouge River** is known throughout most of the world as a basin of industry, site of the massive Ford plant. But in the Detroit area it wears another face. In its upper reaches it is a recreational stream, winding through the west side of the city and several of its suburbs and shaping the terrain into a golfer's delight.

Several of the area's most challenging public courses are situated along the Rouge and its branches.

**Warren Valley Golf Course,** 26116 Warren Road, Dearborn Heights. (313) 561-1040. $39 for 18 holes with cart on weekends; $24 on week days for walkers. From downtown: West on I-96 to southbound Telegraph Road, then left on Warren.

This is one of the oldest courses in the state, designed in 1922 by the famed golf architect Donald Ross. There are 36 holes, many of them playing along the Middle Branch of the Rouge. The river comes into play on seven holes of the west course, and four on the east through generally rolling terrain. The facility is run by Wayne County.

**Inkster Valley Golf Course,** 2150 Middlebelt Road, Inkster. (734) 722-8020. $45 for 18 holes on weekends; $30 on week days. Cart only. From downtown: Take I-94 west to northbound Middlebelt, then on for about 4 miles.

Another county facility, but one at the opposite extreme from Warren Valley. This course, which opened in 1998, was laid out over property that is part of a flood plain and was also used as a dump for many years. Michigan-based architect Harry Bowers, who was accustomed to working on more promising sites in the northern part of the state, managed to utilize the river on most holes while staying clear of the flood plain. It does incorporate 100 acres of wetlands, though.

**Dearborn Hills Golf Course,** 1300 South Telegraph Road, Dearborn. (313) 563-4653. $48.50 on weekends with cart; $24.50 for week days on foot. From downtown: Take I-94 west to northbound Telegraph Road, then on for two miles.

Another historic course, it was built by Robert Herndon, with advice from Walter Hagen, in 1922. A recent redesign added 16 ponds to the layout which plays along the Lower Rouge. It was deeded to the City of Dearborn by Herndon's widow in 1986.

**Rouge Park Golf Course,** 11701 Burt Road, Detroit. (313) 837-5900. $35 weekends with cart; $22 weekdays on foot. From downtown: Take I-96 to southbound Outer Drive, then left on Plymouth Road.

The river runs right through this Detroit course, and it is recommended for novices as a learning experience.

*Another cluster of courses has taken shape around Metro Airport. Odd because the geography is pancake flat in this area; that's why they put the airport there. But developers were smart enough to see that many business travelers prefer to stay at Metro and might be persuaded to play a round if the course was convenient.*

**Gateway Golf Club,** 33290 Gateway Drive, Romulus. (734) 721-4100. $49 on weekends with cart; $44 on weekdays. Two miles north of the airport via Merriman Road and then left on Van Born Road.

A work of inventive genius by Michigan golf architect Jerry Matthews. He was given an empty tract of flat land and told to build a course. His use of ponds is artful, with one island hole and water coming into play on several others. Greens are huge, trees sparse and fairways wide, but it is nonetheless a challenging course and has hosted a number of U.S. Amateur and Michigan PGA events. It is situated amid the largest housing development in the history of Romulus and less than 10 minutes from the airport.

**Lakes of Taylor,** 25505 Northline Road, Taylor.
(734) 287-2100. $55 on weekends with cart; $48 on week-days. Just east of the airport by way of eastbound I-94 to southbound Telegraph Road, then right on Northline.

An unusually fine clubhouse has given this course the slogan, "the public's country club." The course lives up to the billing, too. It is an Arthur Hills design, with lots of little ponds and wetlands sprinkled across it to make the fairly flat terrain a challenge. Woods come into play on the back nine.

**Taylor Meadows Golf Club,** 25360 Ecorse Road, Taylor. (734) 784-4653. $42 with cart at all times. North from the airport on Merriman Rd. and then right on Ecorse Road for about 4 miles.

A very popular course with area golfers because it plays fair. No impossible hazards to bedevil the novice, but some interesting doglegs and rolling terrain on the fairways keep the interest up.

**Woodlands of Van Buren,** 39670 Ecorse Road, Wayne. (734) 729-4477. $53 weekends with cart; $45 on week-days. North on Merriman Road, then left on Ecorse Road for about 5 miles.

Another Jerry Matthews design, with well-conditioned bent grass as a defining feature. The signature hole is the 14th; a 466-yard par 4, guarded by a pond and surrounded by woods. The bunkers also are skillfully placed to test shot-making choices. An exceptionally pleasant dining terrace adds to the ambience.

*Other courses of particular interest would include:*

**Northville Hills,** 15565 Bay Hill Drive, Northville. (734) 667-4653. Weekends with cart $79; weekdays $69. West on I-96 and M-14 to Sheldon Road exit and then right to Five Mile Road. The course is half a mile west on Five Mile.

This is a great big Arnold Palmer designed course (7,003

yards from the back tees), the centerpiece of a residential community in this upscale section of northwestern Wayne County. There are some tricky bunker placements, heather in the roughs and plentiful water hazards, but the greens are exceptionally wide and the fairways forgive many errors.

**Chandler Park,** 12801 Chandler Park Drive, Detroit. (313) 331-7755. Weekends with cart $34; weekdays $30. Take I-94 east to Connor exit. Right to Chandler Park Drive and then left.

A complete remake has turned a rather ordinary city-owned course into a minor masterpiece, operated by American Golf Resorts. New ponds, new bunkers, extended play area, renovated clubhouse. And a dowdy course becomes an urban Cinderella. It is also the only public course on the east side of Detroit.

# AFTER DARK

## *Theater*

The **Fisher** is the top stage in town, the venue for big Broadway road shows and star vehicles. It is located in the Fisher Building, at Second Blvd. and West Grand Blvd., in the New Center area, about 3 miles north of downtown. (313) 872-1000.

**Masonic Temple.** Some of the more elaborate productions play the Masonic Temple because of its larger stage area. It also hosts some dance events and concerts in a hall that was described as the largest Masonic building in North America when it opened in the 1920s. The Masons have since moved out. The Temple is located at Second and Temple, just beyond the northern fringe of the downtown area. (313) 832-7100.

The **Gem and Century Theaters** share a building and put on intimate revues and small shows in a cabaret setting. They are on Madison Ave. at Brush, just one block south of Comerica Park. (313) 963-9800.

The **Music Hall Center for the Performing Arts,** one block to the east on Madison, is also a place where more modest productions, jazz artists and dance troupes play. (313) 963-2366.

The **Detroit Opera House,** at Broadway at Grand Circus Park, is the home of the Michigan Opera Theater and can also accommodate large musical productions. (313) 961-3500.

The **Fox Theatre,** a huge and splendiferous former movie palace, is usually the place for touring Broadway revivals and big name pop and comedy acts. Its Christmas show has become a city tradition and it also is the usual venue for shows aimed for children. It is located at 2211 Woodward. (313) 471-3200.

The **City Theatre** opened in 2004, one block north of the Fox, at 2301 Woodward. It was a space previously occupied by Detroit's Second City ensemble, which moved to the suburbs. The City puts on performance comedy and small shows.

**Wayne State University** has one of the country's finest undergraduate schools of theater. Lily Tomlin, Tom Sizemore, Tom Skerritt, Jeffrey Tambor and many others studied there, and its productions easily rank with professional shows.

Its primary venue is the Bonstelle Theatre, a domed structure which began its life in the early 20th Century as a Jewish temple. Musicals and dramatic revivals make up its season. It is located at 3424 Woodward, between downtown and the Cultural Center. (313) 577-2960.

The smaller **Hilberry Theatre,** on the WSU campus, concentrates on the Classics, Shakespeare and the odd French or British farce. It is at 4743 Cass Ave., one block west of Woodward. (313) 577-2960.

**Detroit Repertory Theatre** has won a devoted following for its cutting-edge dramatic offerings, many of them the works of minority playwrights. It has been operating in a rather desolate neighborhood since 1957 but two generations of supporters have managed to find their way there. It is located at 13103 Woodrow Wilson. From downtown take the Lodge Freeway to the Glendale exit, left for one block to Woodrow Wilson and then right. (313) 868-1347.

## Concert Halls and Arenas

**Orchestra Hall** is an acoustic marvel, one of the finest concert halls in the country. Its design was overseen by Ossip Gabrilowitsch, who accepted the position of music director of the Detroit Symphony Orchestra in 1919 on the provision that a suitable hall was built for it. So eager was the city to sign the illustrious pianist that it managed to put the hall up in a bit more than four months. The architect was Howard Crane, the same man who designed the Fox and several more of Detroit's classic movie houses.

The Symphony decided to move out after 20 years and this became the Paradise Theatre, one of the great halls for black jazz artists through the 1940s. From swing to bebop, Ella Fitzgerald to Dizzy Gillespie, they all played the Paradise.

In 1951 the theater closed, however, and stood deserted for many years. The Symphony had moved on to the Ford Auditorium on the riverfront, but there were complaints about acoustics from the day that hall opened.

In the late 1970s, within days of its scheduled demolition, Orchestra Hall was saved through a public fund-raising campaign. It underwent a restoration, relying on old drawings and photographs to bring it back to its original appearance. The Symphony decided to return here in 1989 and it has remained ever since.

The name of the building was officially changed to the Max M. Fisher Music Center in 2003 and it is now incorporated within a larger complex funded by the local philanthropist. It is still the home of the Symphony as well as several other musical and theatrical events. The location is 3711 Woodward Avenue, between downtown and the Cultural Center. (313) 576-5111.

The **State Theatre** is usually a place where rock artists perform. It is another of the city's resplendent old movie houses, one block south of the Fox, at 2115 Woodward. (313) 961-5450.

**Majestic Theatre** is one of the more eclectic locations in town. Within its walls are a Mediterranean-style restaurant, a billiards hall, a bowling alley (reputed to be the oldest in Detroit) and a stage upon which you are likely to find folk, jazz or rock artists. (313) 833-9700.

**Harpo's Concert Theatre** is an East Side stronghold for new rock bands and groups with strong local followings. It's located at 14238 Harper. Take I-94 east to the Chalmers exit, left and then another immediate left on Harper. (313) 824-1700.

**Cobo Arena,** part of the convention center, hosts the occasional pop or rock concert. It seats about 11,000 for most events. It is located at Washington Blvd. at West Jefferson. (313) 983-6616.

**Joe Louis Arena** is home to hockey's Detroit Red Wings as well as a few big name musical acts. It can seat upwards of 20,000. The Joe, as it is known locally, is immediately west of Cobo Arena. (313) 471-6606.

## Music Clubs

**Baker's Keyboard Lounge** is one of the jazz landmarks of America. All the greats have performed here from the 1950s on. While its founder, Clarence Baker, has passed from the scene, it remains a place that honors the past and listens to the present, too. Baker's is located at the north end of the city, at 20510 Livernois, just south of Eight Mile Road. Take the Lodge Freeway to Livernois, turn right and continue for about three miles. (313) 345-6300.

**Portofino's** has become a good stop for music in the Downriver area. The restaurant's location on the Detroit River, in downtown Wyandotte, makes it a rather nice romantic rendezvous. It's at 3455 Biddle. (734) 281-6700.

There is also late-night jazz at **Sweet Georgia Brown,** described in the Restaurant section. (313) 965-1245.

The older suburb of **Hamtramck** has reinvented itself as one of the livelier bar scenes for local bands and alternative rock groups. This is where the locals go to check out tomorrow's breakthrough acts.

Three places to try are **Small's, Paycheck's** and the **New Dodge.** Times and performers vary wildly so check by phone or pick up a copy of the *Metro Times*, the area's alternative weekly and an unmatched source for information on musical events in the city.

**Small's** is located at 10339 Conant, a street that parallels Hamtramck's main drag, Joseph Campau, a few blocks to the east. (313) 873-1117.

**Paycheck's** is at 2932 Caniff. (313) 874-0254.

The **New Dodge** is at 5963 Joseph Campau. (313) 874-5963.

# CASINOS

Detroit has three major casinos, located downtown or immediately outside the central core. All of them have plans to expand and add 500-room hotels. As of this writing, however, all these plans remain on paper as casino management and politicians argue about the details. When it does happen, it will be big.

All are open 24 hours daily. The lounges feature local acts rather than stars, although if you look closely you may catch a big name in for a one-nighter. All of them have the usual; craps, slots and the standard card games. No sports book.

**MGM Grand** is on the west side of downtown, just off the Lodge Freeway, at the Howard Street exit. There are

*Lots of slots right this way*

2,700 slots, 80 table games, four restaurants, buffet, live entertainment at the Stage Bar. Hollywood theme. A touch of irony: The site used to be the Detroit office of the Internal Revenue Service. (877) 888-2121.

**Motor City Casino** is just to the north, off the Lodge at the Grand River exit. There are 2,500 slots here, 83 tables, four restaurants. Live entertainment at the Overdrive Lounge. Automotive theme. Another touch of irony: This used to be a bread factory. (313) 237-7711.

**Greektown Casino** is on the east side of downtown, in the Greektown area. Exit I-375 at East Lafayette and turn right. Newspaper reader polls keep naming this as the favorite casino in town, so they must be doing something right. There are 2,500 slots, 99 tables, three lounges and restaurants. Naturally, a Greek theme. Not so ironic note. This used to be an indoor shopping mall. (888) 771-4386.

*The city's liveliest corner by night*

**Casino Windsor** is for those who want to see how it feels to lose their money in a foreign country. Take the Tunnel from downtown, right at the exit, left to Riverside Drive and then straight ahead. You'll find 3,300 slots, 86 tables and an attached hotel. No quibbling with local government about that because the casino is operated by the Province of Ontario. (800) 991-7777.

## Movies

**General Motors** has announced plans to reopen the theaters in the **RenCen** in 2005. They had been closed since the early 90s and will become the first downtown movie location to operate since that time. The next closest choice is the **Star Fairlane,** in Dearborn's Fairlane Town Center, Michigan Ave. at the Southfield Freeway. (313) 240-6389.

Some other major cineplexes are the **AMC Livonia 20,** at Haggerty and Seven Mile roads, just off I-275. (734) 542-9909.

The **Showcase Dearborn,** at Michigan Ave. and Telegraph Road. (313) 561-3449.

The **Phoenix Bel-Air Centre,** Detroit, on East Eight Mile Road, east of Van Dyke. (313) 438-3494.

The **Emagine Canton,** at 39535 Ford Road, just east of I-75. (888) 319-3456.

The **Detroit Film Theatre** presents an outstanding selection of offbeat offerings, foreign movies, revivals and stuff that simply deserves a second look. Its season usually runs only on weekends but the schedule varies. The DFT screens its films within the Detroit Institute of Arts. Call (313) 833-3237 for schedule and directions.

# BEST WITH KIDS

*Vintage cars at Greenfield Village*

1. The Greenfield Village section of the Henry Ford is an historical theme park that gives kids a chance to run around outside, too.
2. Older kids will appreciate the Rouge Plant tours.
3. The IMAX Theatre in the New Detroit Science Center is a good bet and so are the hands-on exhibits there.
4. Take a ride on the People Mover
5. Visit the streets of Old Detroit section of the Detroit Historical Museum.
6. Walk through GM World and look at the new vehicles in the RenCen.
7. Take the behind-the-scenes tour of Ford Field, home of the Detroit Lions.

# ANNUAL EVENTS

*January:*

**North American International Auto Show.** This is the city's annual over-the-top blowout, an extravaganza that glorifies the new models, both vehicular and human, from the industry that defines Detroit. Always packed and always fun. Usually held the second full week of the month at Cobo Convention Center in downtown Detroit. Call (313) 877-8777.

*Crowds pack the annual auto show*

**Plymouth International Ice Sculpture Spectacular.** It's winter and you might as well have some fun with it. Sculptors carve out fanciful and unlikely designs from huge blocks of ice which are then displayed in Plymouth's downtown park. Dates vary. Call (734) 453-1540.

*February:*

**Black History Month** is always observed with month-long special exhibits at the Charles H. Wright Museum of African-American History and at the Henry Ford, in Dearborn. Other cultural events go on at theaters throughout the area.

**Detroit Boat Show.** With the Great Lakes all around, thousands of inland lakes and the Detroit River at its doorstep, this area is wild about the water. This annual exhibit shows off the latest ideas in watercraft and all the other things that go with it. Usually in the second full week of the month, at the Cobo Convention Center. (734) 261-0123.

## May:

**Movement.** Detroit's Electronic Music Festival. From a modest beginning, this has grown into an internationally recognized event, with cutting-edge groups from around the world coming to Hart Plaza to perform. Last weekend of the month. (313) 567-0080.

**Budweiser Downtown Hoedown.** The big city goes Country in this bash at Hart Plaza. Major acts appear in Motown's annual salute to Nashville. Call the CVB for details at (800) 338-7648.

**Greektown Arts Festival.** An annual street fair in one of downtown's cheeriest corners, along Monroe St. between Beaubien and St. Antoine. Call (313) 963-3357 for dates.

## June:

**Detroit Festival of the Arts.** This is when the folks in the Cultural Center get to do their thing, from music to arts and crafts. Second weekend of the month. (313) 577-5088.

**Comerica Tastefest.** An annual celebration of food and its many delights, held along West Grand Blvd. in the New Center area. Local restaurants set up booths for passers-by to sample their wares. Last weekend of the month. (313) 872-0188.

**International Freedom Festival and Marshall Field's Target Fireworks.** A very big deal, indeed, coinciding with Canada Day, on July 1, and the Fourth of July. The festival is a joint U.S.-Canadian celebration of the peaceful border and shared democratic values. More than a million people pour into the downtown areas of Detroit and Windsor to gape at one of North America's great fireworks shows. Riverfront hotels are sold out a year in advance and people arrive eight hours early to stake out a prime viewing area. The fireworks usually go off on the last Wednesday in June. Many more musical and cultural events are scheduled on both sides of the border. Call (313) 923-8259 for a schedule.

## *July:*

**Gold Cup Hydroplane Races.** One of the great events in powerboat racing and a summertime tradition in Detroit. The course runs along the riverfront, east of the Belle Isle Bridge. Dates vary. Call (586) 774-1711.

## *August:*

**Michigan State Fair.** It's the oldest in the country and while the Fairgrounds are located within Detroit, it still has that country feel; with agricultural exhibits, corn dogs, a midway and name entertainment. The Fairgrounds are located at Woodward and Eight Mile Road. The last two weeks of August.
(313) 369-8250.

**African World Festival.** A celebration of the many strands of African culture in the Detroit area. Music, dance, crafts, food. At Hart Plaza, third weekend of the month.
(313) 494-5824.

## *September:*

**International Jazz Festival.** The city has deep roots in the jazz tradition and honors the art form over Labor Day weekend. Some of the biggest names in the field turn up to perform at both free and ticketed events. Call (313) 963-2366 for a schedule.

## *November:*

**Wayne County Lightfest.** The holiday season begins when this four-mile long illuminated roadway lights up. It is billed as the Midwest's biggest Christmas show, with animated displays and nearly one million lights. It runs along Hines Drive, a parkway that parallels the Rouge River. Best point of entry is at Merriman Road, in Westland. It begins in mid-November and runs through January 1. (734) 261-1990.

**America's Thanksgiving Parade.** Another grand Detroit tradition, as floats and marching bands make their way down Woodward Ave. and Santa makes his annual arrival. Once sponsored by the erstwhile J.L. Hudson Department Store, it is now a community effort put on by the Parade Company, which was specifically formed to save this event—and what a great job they've done. Some of the city's most noted celebrities appear as clowns. It starts off at 10 a.m. Thanksgiving morning. (313) 923-7400.

## *December:*

**The Edsel and Eleanor Ford House.** In Grosse Pointe Shores, puts on a series of traditional holiday events---teas and caroling---throughout the month. (313) 884-4222.